Fulton Books, Inc.
Meadville, PA

Published by Fulton Books 2021

ISBN 978-1-63985-002-0 (paperback)
ISBN 978-1-63985-878-1 (hardcover)
ISBN 978-1-63985-003-7 (digital)

Printed in the United States of America

# Feathers the House Duck

Beverlee McFadden

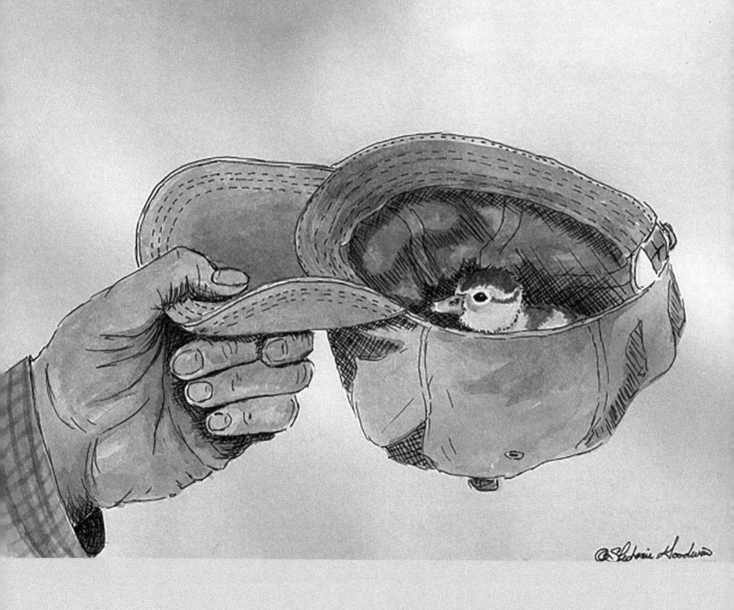

# Chapter 1

One cool foggy morning, Farmer Joe went outside to do chores. He was on his way to feed the cows, but first, he headed to the barn to turn out the chickens and ducks.

As he was about to open the gate, he noticed that all the farm cats were in a group staring at something in the grass. He went to check it out and discovered a *tiny duckling*, which was scared to death.

Farmer Joe snatched up the tiny duckling and put it in his hat, then headed back to the house. As he opened the door, he yelled to his wife, "Hilda, come here, I have something for you." Hilda was in the middle of making bread, so she washed her hands, and as she was drying them, she went to Joe. He held out his hat for her to see. She exclaimed, "Joe, that's a Muscovy duckling, where did you find it?" As he explained to her where he found the duckling, Hilda got a box, a towel, and containers for water and feed. Joe placed the duckling in the box, and they both went back to their chores of feeding animals and baking bread.

Over the next few days, they both kept watching to see if any more ducklings would show up, but after a week, there was still just the one little duckling. This presented quite a problem. Ducklings need companions to grow and thrive. If there aren't any, they will latch on to anything or anybody that are around. Since Hilda and Joe were the only ones that the duckling saw, they became the duckling's companions.

That is how the little duckling became a house duck.

# Chapter 2

Joe and Hilda took care of the duckling's needs, and the little duckling grew and grew. It grew so much that it grew out of the box. Joe brought in a large plastic container that was big enough to last until the duckling grew to full size.

The duckling was beginning to grow small feathers on its wings and tail. One day, Hilda decided it was time for the duckling to stretch its legs and took the duckling out of the plastic container and set the duckling on the kitchen floor.

The duckling took off running in circles, not knowing where to go, but soon started exploring the kitchen area. It came across a mousetrap that was on the floor by the refrigerator. The little duckling touched it and *snap*! It scared the little duck, and it backed away, then it went to the other side of the refrigerator, and there was another mousetrap, *snap*! That one almost got the duckling. That was the end of exploring mousetraps.

Hilda and Joe have two long-haired dogs that stay in the house quite a bit, and as long as the duckling was contained, the dogs didn't mind it, but that long hair on the dog's tail was like a magnet to the duckling. Just like a two-year-old child, the duckling took a mouthful of hair and ran.

The dog yipped and barked at the little duck, and Hilda scolded the dog. That was all it took for the duckling to know how to deal with the dogs.

# Chapter 3

There was always a pan of dry dog food on the floor for the dogs to eat, and the duckling discovered that if you drop a piece of dog food, it rolls, then you can chase it, pick it up, drop it again, and chase it. This game went on for quite a while. Watching a duck run is quite a sight. Those flat flipper feet do go fast that they get tangled up, and the little duck can fall head over feet so fast, it wonders what happened.

One morning, Hilda was at the kitchen sink, and the sun was shining on the duckling and the feathers were shining. That was the day the little duckling got its name Feathers.

By now, Feathers was four months old and old enough to tell if it was a boy or a girl duck. Hilda always thought it was a boy, or drake in duck terms, but it turned out, Feathers was a girl, or hen in duck terms. She will lay eggs as soon as she is old enough. That happens at about six months old. It would be two more months before she would lay her first egg. That will be an exciting day, but first, she had more growing and exploring to do.

Feathers still stayed in the large container at night and was fully feathered by now. Learning how to flap and control the feathers for flight was something she had been working on for weeks.

One morning, just as Hilda went to the kitchen, Feathers jumped so high and flapped her wings that she flew out of the container and landed on the dinner table. Hilda was shocked, but Feathers was so proud of her accomplishment that Hilda just grabbed her and placed her on the floor, thinking, *My little girl is growing up.*

# Chapter 4

By now, Feathers had roamed all over and knew the layout of the house. She would follow Joe and Hilda everywhere and would join in whatever was going on. She was a member of the family. She would sit on laps as they watched TV or play with the paper as Joe tried to read it.

But the day she pushed all the buttons on the remote, she got into trouble. It took Joe over an hour to figure out how to get the television working again. But Feathers didn't seem to mind. After all, she's just a duck.

Not long after her first flight, she was in the kitchen minding her own business and accidently got her foot stepped on. She screamed and yelled and screamed some more. The next few days, she stayed in her container, keeping far away from feet. Gradually day after day, she improved and was ready to join the family again. Since she had learned how to fly, she would flap those wings and hop on her good leg. Doing this, she could manage to travel around the house. Then as she improved she had a bad limp, but days later, she was as good as new. She was now ready for her next adventure.

# Chapter 5

Muscovy ducks don't quack like other ducks. They make a peeping sound, but ever since Feathers was a duckling, she has chirped like a bird, then it turned to a whistle. As she got older, she would make a sound like the squeak of the clothes dryer. She could mimic the sounds she would hear every day.

At Christmas, when the family was together at the farm, Hilda thought the dogs were outside barking. She went to the window and looked out, but there were no dogs. She thought she must have been hearing things. Hours later as everyone was leaving, her son said, "I think Feathers just barked!" So it was confirmed, Feathers can bark like a dog.

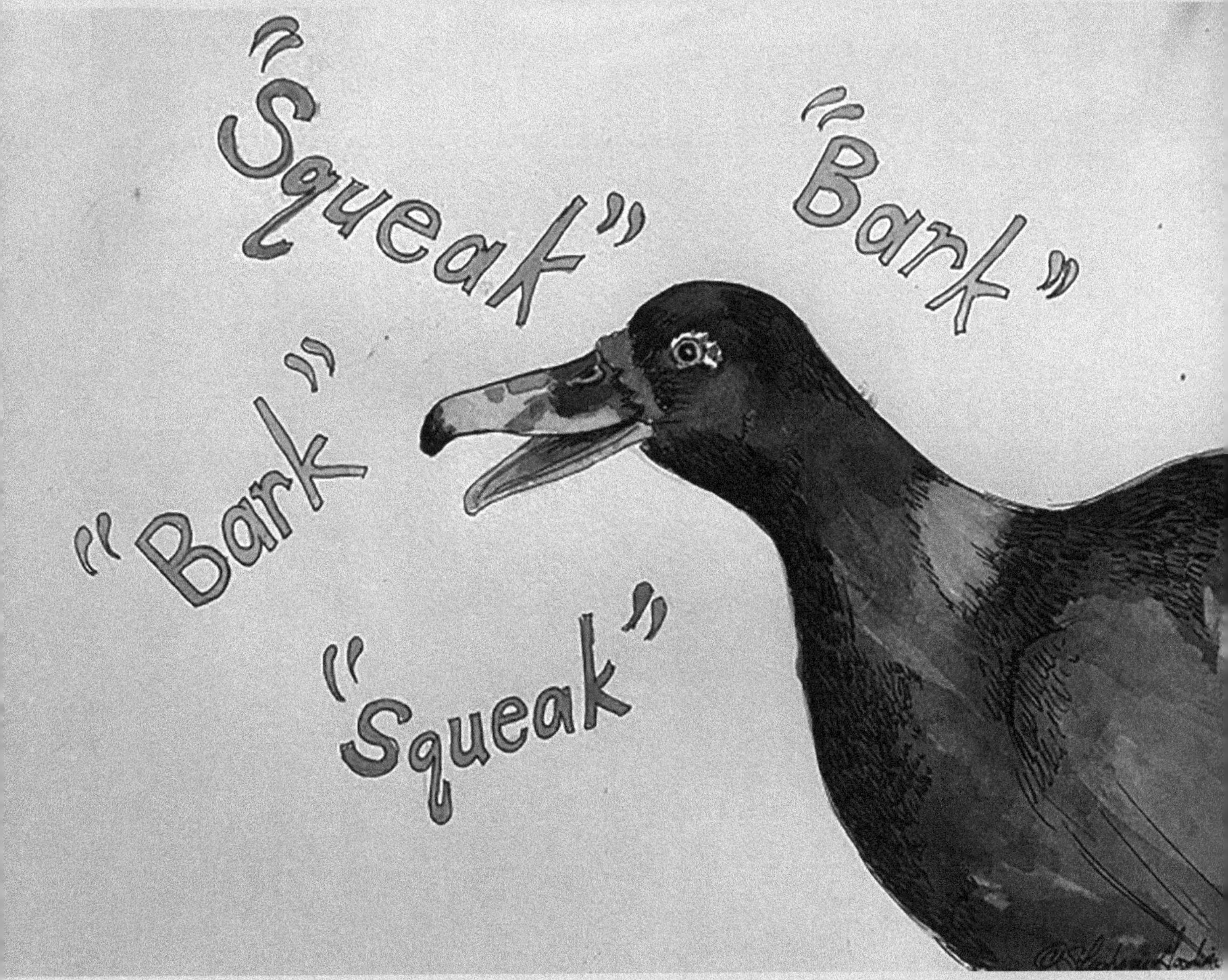
"Squeak"
"Bark"
"Bark"
"Squeak"

As the days went on, Feathers seemed to enjoy the human world. She would play with objects she would find lying around the house, a pencil, a stick that the dogs brought in, or the brush attachment from the vacuum sweeper that she somehow managed to get out of the holder. That brush seemed to have legs because it managed to make it into every room in the house. Hilda wondered if Feathers thought she was helping to clean because it was hard for Feathers to push the brush across the floor. But I guess we will never really know.

# Chapter 6

Every morning after Hilda would get out of bed, she would pull the covers over the bed. Feathers would be waiting in the bedroom, looking in the full-length mirror at herself. Feathers would try to figure out who or what she was. She would look and look, and, when she moved, so would the thing in the mirror. As long as Hilda would stay in the bedroom, Feathers would look in the mirror and stare at herself. But when Hilda was finished and headed down the hall, Feathers would follow with the *thump*, *thump*, *thump* of those flat duck feet pounding the floor all the way down the hall.

One day, the whole family came out to the farm, including their dog Hank. Hilda and Joe's grandson was holding Feathers. Hank and Feathers tolerate each other, but both have an eye out to create trouble. Hank all of a sudden saw Feathers and lunged at the duck, which flapped her wings to get away and ended up on top of the grandson's head. Talk about a commotion! It took the whole family to grab Hank and Feathers to rescue their grandson from bodily harm. Hank got put outside because Feathers needed some time to cool down. All in all, everything turned out okay.

# Chapter 7

By now, winter was on its way out, and spring is on its way in. Snow had fallen, and much-needed rain had come. Feathers had grown up to a mature Muscovy hen. She had some not so pleasant habits over her time with the family.

She taught them to leave their shoes and socks on because to her, toes look like worms. If she got a hold of a toe with her bill, she would bite down with all her strength and pinch the toe. *"Ouch!"*

With spring came lots of changes. One change is molting that occurs with poultry. This is the time that ducks and chickens loose old feathers and grow new ones. It's just part of their life. It seems to be that time for Feathers now. In the house, there were feathers everywhere. Hilda tried to keep them swept up, but Feathers seemed to prefer them scattered all over. Hilda swept the feathers into a pile, and before she can pick them up, Feathers flapped those wings and scattered them all over again. This happened twice, and Feathers was put in another room to eliminate it happening a third time.

One evening, Hilda and Joe sat down to relax after a long day of work. Joe thought it would good to find a movie to watch on TV. He turned on the TV, and Hilda sat back in the recliner and put her feet up, getting real comfortable, and then the doorbell rang. She flipped the handle on the recliner to lower the foot stand so she could get up and go to the door. When she came back, she sat back down in the recliner and heard something like a dog barking outside, so she got up again to look out the window, but as she turned, she noticed the sound was coming from the chair. *Oh dear*, she thought and reached for the handle, raised the foot, and Feathers shot out from under the recliner, went about four feet, stopped, turned around, and started chattering in duck talk right at Hilda. Feathers was not happy with what she had just been through and was telling Hilda all about it. It was a few days before Feathers would let Hilda even touch her, but things were forgotten a little later and the two made up.

# Chapter 8

The days were warming now, and Feathers enjoyed going outside for fresh air and sunshine just as long as someone was with her. This was all new to Feathers since she had grown up in the house and didn't know the outside existed. She had a lot of exploring to do. At first, she didn't want to leave the deck. But as she got used to it, she would inch her way little by little until she managed to touch dirt. This was a whole new ball game for her. She could make footprints in the dirt and would run around flapping her wings, making all kinds of designs in the dry soil. Hilda laughed and laughed watching her explore her new surroundings.

One day, Feathers noticed something green in the dirt. It was a weed. Hilda saw her look at it strangely, so Hilda picked it, grabbed Feathers, and went back into the house. Hilda placed the weed in Feather's food bowl, hoping Feathers would get the idea that it was food and give it a try. It worked! Feathers gobbled it up and enjoyed it. Every time Feathers was outside, she would look for little green weed and eat them. This is what Hilda was hoping Feathers would do. Every time Hilda went out with Feathers, she noticed that the farm ducks would walk back and forth along the fence, trying to get a glimpse of what Feathers was doing. Feathers never looked up once because her main interest was looking for those yummy weeds.

It was now the month of March, and gardening would be here before long. Hilda and Joe always put out a large vegetable garden. They grew enough vegetables to last about a year. So with gardening, you need to start with seeds that you will plant out in the garden to grow the food. Hilda and her son spent days deciding what to grow and then went to work planting tiny seeds into little pots. This is not a job that Hilda likes, but it's an important part of gardening.

They placed the many containers of potted seeds in Joe and Hilda's bay window. With the warm sun coming in the window, it wasn't long until the seed sprouted and start to grow. That is one thing that Hilda enjoys. She loves to watch the little sprouts grow into plants.

One morning Hilda was sitting in her recliner drinking her coffee and noticed some soil on the shelf of the bay window. She discovered that some of her seedlings were gone! It looked like something or someone had helped themselves to the little plants. Feathers had pulled up and ate the seedlings. Hilda was furious. She scolded Feathers for eating them. Then Joe reminded her that she was the one that showed Feathers what to do with the weeds. Feathers was just doing what she had been taught only this time it was Hilda that learned something.

When Feathers would go out into the backyard, the farm ducks would walk the fence looking at Feathers, then one day the only mallard on the farm, who is named Samantha, jumped and flew over the fence. She went right up to Feathers and introduced herself. Hilda watched as Samantha and Feathers walked side by side across the yard. Their bills were moving up and down, talking to each other. They had become friends.

Every day after that when Feathers was outside, Samantha would fly over the fence and visit with Feathers for a time and then fly back over the fence and go home.

As time went by, Feathers would spend her days outside more and more. She explored things in the yard, which was a common thing for her to do. She enjoyed the outdoors but always wanted Hilda or Joe to be within sight.

One day, she and both the dogs were out in the yard. The dogs went back in the house after about thirty minutes, leaving Feathers all alone. It wasn't long before there was a tap, tap, tap on

the door. So Hilda opened the door, and Feathers walked in. She had watched the dogs scratch the door to be let back in the house. Feathers learned by watching the dogs.

The very next morning after everyone was up, Hilda and Joe were getting ready to drink their coffee. Joe looked down at this chair, and there was a newly laid egg. Feathers had laid her first egg. Exactly seven months to the day when Feathers hatched from hers.

36

## About the Author

Beverelee McFadden was born and raised in southwest Kansas. After graduating from high school, she attended DCCC in Dodge City where she met her husband. They got married, had two boys, and still live on the family farm at Minneola, Kansas. They raise cattle and have chickens and ducks, and that is how this story came about.

Stephanie Goodwin lives in Kearney, Nebraska. She lived most of her life in Kansas. She went to Fort Hays State University in Hays, Kansas, where she majored in art education and minored in business. She taught for twenty-eight years in Atwood, Kansas. Eighteen of those year were spent teaching elementary art. This book is a collaboration with her sister Beverlee.